# *Parisian Bistro Delights*
# TASTES OF FRANCE

A Journey Through Timeless French Recipes: Discover the Charm of Authentic Bistro Cuisine in Every Bite.

# JAMES STOTT

Dear future culinary adventurers and cooking enthusiasts, as you embark on the flavorful journey within the pages of this book, we would like to extend a warm invitation for you to share your thoughts with us.
Posting a review or leaving a star rating review would be really appreciated and can be accessed using the link via the QR code here.

To be kept informed of any new cookbook releases and future book promotions please drop an email with your name to:

For cookbooks, email Cookbooks@SoReadyToRead.com

For crime books, email Crime@SoReadyToRead.com

For personal development books,
email Development@SoReadyToRead.com

For technology, blockchain, and their uses books, email Technology@SoReadyToRead.com

To receive notifications for all book genres, send an email with your name to All@soreadytoread.com

Review Tastes of France

# Introduction

Welcome to "Bistro Bliss: Tastes of France," where every page turned is a step deeper into the heart of French culinary traditions. France, with its rich history and diverse landscapes, has long been celebrated not just for its contributions to art, fashion, and culture, but also for its timeless culinary traditions. This book seeks to celebrate the latter – the bustling bistros dotted across its cities and the authentic, heartwarming dishes they serve.

Bistros, often tucked away in the winding alleys of Paris or the sun-kissed streets of Provence, have always been more than just eateries. They are places where stories unfold, romances blossom, and the charm of France comes alive in every plate presented. This book aims to bring that very charm right to your kitchen. Whether you're a seasoned chef or someone just embarking on their culinary journey, "Bistro Bliss" offers a treasure trove of recipes that cater to all.

From the crisp crust of Tarte Flambee to the aromatic allure of Ratatouille Niçoise, this cookbook has been curated to ensure that every dish you make transports you and your loved ones straight to a cozy corner bistro in France. Each recipe, while rooted deeply in tradition, has been designed to be recreated in contemporary kitchens, ensuring that the essence of the bistro experience remains uncompromised.

As you journey through this book, you'll not only discover classic dishes that have been passed down through generations but also the stories, traditions, and techniques that make French bistro cuisine an art in itself. Every ingredient, every simmer, every bake has a tale to tell. And now, it's your turn to be a part of that tale.

So, tie on your apron, preheat that oven, and embark on a gastronomic adventure that promises to be as fulfilling as it is delicious. Let's discover the charm, passion, and elegance of authentic bistro cuisine in every bite.

Bon Appétit!

# Contents

Introduction........................................................................3

**French Cuisine** .................................................................**7**

Tarte Flambee (Alsatian Pizza)...........................................9

Roasted Camembert With Garlic And Herbs ......................11

Grilled Sardines With Lemon And Olive Oil .......................13

Beef Tartare With Capers And Cornichons ........................15

Lentil Salad With Walnuts And Goat Cheese .....................17

Gratin De Chou-Fleur (Cauliflower Gratin) ........................19

Flamiche (Leek Tart) .........................................................21

Moules Marinières (Mussels In White Wine) .....................23

Ratte Potatoes With Herbs De Provence ...........................25

Spinach And Gruyère Soufflé ............................................27

Salade De Lentilles (Lentil Salad) .....................................29

Brandade De Morue (Salt Cod And Potato Purée) ..............31

Rabbit In Mustard Sauce ..................................................33

Rôti De Porc Au Lait (Pork Roast With Milk) .....................35

Tarte Au Maroilles (Maroilles Cheese Tart) .......................37

Tarte Normande (Apple Custard Tart) ...............................39

Endive And Ham Gratin ....................................................41

Grilled Trout With Almonds ..............................................43

Cream Of Chestnut Soup ..................................................45

Rabbit Terrine With Pistachios .........................................47

Ratatouille Niçoise ...........................................................49

Cervelle De Canut (Herbed Cheese Spread) ......................51

Flaugnarde (Berry Clafoutis) ............................................53

Petits Farçis Niçois (Stuffed Vegetables) ..........................55

Pan Bagnat (Provençal Tuna Sandwich) ...........................57

Chèvre Chaud Sur Toast ............................................................ 59

Brioche French Toast With Lavender Honey ............................ 61

Mont D'or Au Four (Baked Mont D'or Cheese) ....................... 63

Tournedos Rossini (Beef With Foie Gras) .............................. 65

Galette Complète ....................................................................... 67

Tartine Provençale ..................................................................... 69

Salade De Mâche (Lamb's Lettuce Salad) .............................. 71

Smoked Salmon Quiche............................................................ 73

Duck Breast With Cherry Sauce............................................... 75

Lamb Navarin ............................................................................. 77

Veal Blanquette (Veal In White Sauce) ................................... 79

Buckwheat Crepes With Ham And Cheese............................. 81

Grilled Mussels With Parsley And Garlic ................................ 83

Red Snapper With Tomato And Olives..................................... 85

**Dessert.............................................................................. 87**

Figs Roasted With Honey And Thyme ..................................... 89

Pâte De Fruits (Fruit Jellies) .................................................... 91

Red Wine Poached Pears ......................................................... 93

Mousse Au Chocolat Noir ......................................................... 95

Caramelized Shallot Tart........................................................... 97

Madeleines (French Sponge Cakes)........................................ 99

Paris-Brest (Choux Pastry With Praline Cream) ................... 101

Potatoes Anna (Layered Potato Cake) .................................. 103

Meringues With Whipped Cream............................................ 105

Cherry Clafoutis...................................................................... 107

Chocolate And Almond Torte ................................................. 109

Conclusion .............................................................................. 110

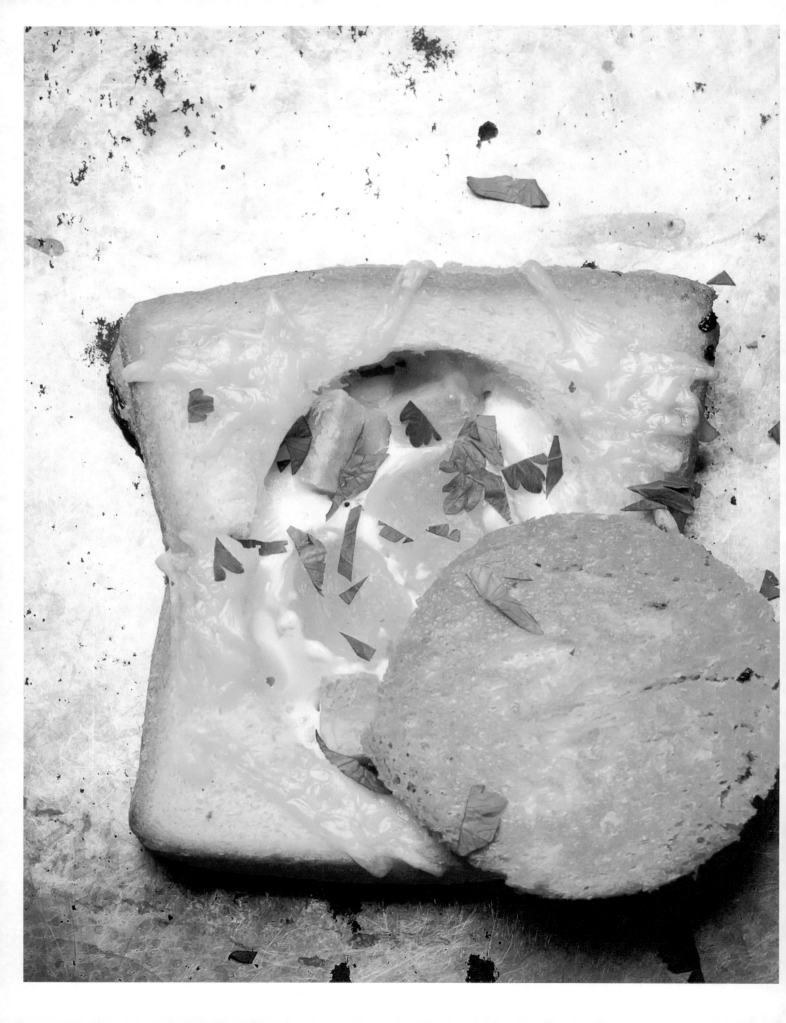

FRENCH CUISINE

# TARTE FLAMBEE (ALSATIAN PIZZA)

**Prep Time:**
2 hour 30 mins

**Cook Time:**
15 mins

**Serving**
4-6

**Nutrition:**   Calories: 450, Fat: 18g, Carbohydrates: 58g, Fiber: 2g, Protein: 14g

| INGREDIENTS | PREPARATIONS |
|---|---|
| For the Dough:<br>2 1/4 cups all-purpose flour<br>1 teaspoon salt<br>1 tablespoon sugar<br>1 tablespoon active dry yeast<br>1 cup warm water<br>For the Topping:<br>1 cup crème fraîche or sour cream<br>1 large onion, thinly sliced<br>8 ounces of lardons or chopped bacon<br>Salt and pepper to taste<br>A pinch of nutmeg | 1. In a large-sized bowl, combine the flour, salt, and sugar. Mix the yeast with the warm water in a separate bowl and let it sit for a few minutes until it becomes frothy.<br>2. Pour the yeast into the flour mixture until it forms a ball. Knead the dough on a floured surface for about 5 minutes until it's smooth and elastic. Grease a bowl and add the dough inside. Cover it with a kitchen towel and leave it to rise for approximately 2 hours until it has doubled. Adjust the oven to 450 degrees F (232 degrees C) and place a pizza stone or an upside-down baking sheet inside.<br>3. First, divide the dough into four parts. Then, roll each portion out on a floured surface until it becomes very thin.<br>4. Spread a thin layer of crème fraîche on each piece of dough, leaving a small border around the edges. Top with sliced onions and lardons—season with salt, pepper, and a sprinkle of nutmeg.<br>5. Slide one of the tarts onto the oven's preheated stone or cooking sheet using a pizza peel or another upside-down baking sheet. Prepare for 12-15 minutes until the crust is golden and the toppings are bubbling.<br>6. Repeat with the remaining tarts, and serve hot. |

# ROASTED CAMEMBERT WITH GARLIC AND HERBS

**Prep Time:**
**10 mins**

**Cook Time:**
**20 mins**

**Serving**
**2-4**

**Nutrition:**   Calories: 290, Fat: 23g, Carbohydrates: 1g, Fiber: 0g, Protein: 18g

| INGREDIENTS | PREPARATIONS |
|---|---|
| 1 wheel of Camembert cheese<br>2 cloves of garlic, thinly sliced<br>2 sprigs of fresh thyme<br>1 sprig of fresh rosemary<br>2 tablespoons olive oil<br>Salt and pepper to taste | 1. Set your oven's temperature to 350 degrees F (180 degrees C).<br>2. Place the Camembert in a small baking dish. Make several small slits on top of the cheese with a sharp knife.<br>3. Insert the slices of garlic, thyme, and rosemary sprigs into the slits.<br>4. Drizzle the oil over the cheese and season with salt and pepper.<br>5. Bake for 20 minutes or until the cheese is soft and melted. Serve with crusty bread. |

# GRILLED SARDINES WITH LEMON AND OLIVE OIL

**Prep Time:**
**10 mins**

**Cook Time:**
**6 mins**

**Serving**
**4**

**Nutrition:**   Calories: 250, Fat: 18g, Carbohydrates: 3g, Fiber: 1g, Protein: 20g

| INGREDIENTS | PREPARATIONS |
|---|---|
| 12 fresh sardines, cleaned and gutted<br>4 tablespoons olive oil<br>2 lemons, halved<br>Salt and pepper to taste | 1. Set your grill or barbecue to medium heat.<br>2. Rinse the sardines under cold water and pat them dry with a paper towel.<br>3. Brush the sardines using olive oil and season with salt and pepper.<br>4. Grill the sardines for about 3 minutes on each side until the skin is crisp and the fish is cooked through.<br>5. Squeeze fresh lemon juice over the grilled sardines before serving. |

# BEEF TARTARE WITH CAPERS AND CORNICHONS

**Prep Time:**
**20 mins**

**Cook Time:**
**00 mins**

**Serving**
**4**

**Nutrition:** Calories: 480, Fat: 38g, Carbohydrates: 2g, Fiber: 0g, Protein: 30g

| INGREDIENTS | PREPARATIONS |
|---|---|
| 500g high quality, fresh beef fillet, minced<br>1 small red onion, finely chopped<br>2 tablespoons capers, rinsed and chopped<br>4 cornichons, finely chopped<br>4 tablespoons olive oil<br>Salt and black pepper to taste<br>4 free-range egg yolks | 1. Combine the minced beef, red onion, capers, cornichons, and olive oil in a large-sized mixing bowl. Season with salt and black pepper. Mix until well combined.<br>2. Divide the beef tartare into 4 equal portions. Shape each piece into a patty and make a small well in the center. Place the patties on serving plates.<br>3. Gently place an egg yolk in the well of each beef tartare patty.<br>4. Serve right away with crusty bread and a green salad. |

# LENTIL SALAD WITH WALNUTS AND GOAT CHEESE

**Prep Time:**
**10 mins**

**Cook Time:**
**30 mins**

**Serving**
**4**

**Nutrition:**  Calories: 350, Fat: 18g, Carbohydrates: 30g, Fiber: 12g, Protein: 20g

| INGREDIENTS | PREPARATIONS |
|---|---|
| 1 cup French green lentils<br>2 cups water<br>1 bay leaf<br>2 tablespoons red wine vinegar<br>1 small red onion, finely chopped<br>1/3 cup chopped walnuts<br>4 ounces goat cheese, crumbled<br>1/4 cup chopped fresh parsley<br>Salt and black pepper to taste | 1. Rinse the lentils under cold water and drain. Mix the lentils, water, and bay leaf in a normal-sized saucepan. Take to a boil, then turn the heat to low and simmer for 25-30 minutes until the lentils are tender. Drain and discard the bay leaf.<br>2. Whisk the red wine vinegar, onion, and olive oil in a large bowl. Add the warm lentils to the bowl and toss to combine.<br>3. Let the lentil blend cool to room temperature, then add the walnuts, goat cheese, and parsley. Use salt and pepper to taste, then mix everything carefully.<br>4. Serve at room temperature or chilled. |

# GRATIN DE CHOU-FLEUR (CAULIFLOWER GRATIN)

**Prep Time:
15 mins**

**Cook Time:
30 mins**

**Serving
4**

**Nutrition:**   Calories: 365, Fat: 25g, Carbohydrates: 20g, Fiber: 3g, Protein: 17g

| INGREDIENTS | PREPARATIONS |
|---|---|
| 1 large head cauliflower, cut into florets<br>3 tablespoons unsalted butter<br>3 tablespoons all-purpose flour<br>2 cups milk<br>Salt and black pepper to taste<br>1 cup shredded Gruyère cheese<br>1/2 cup grated Parmesan cheese | 1. Adjust the oven's temperature to 375°F (190°C).<br>2. Boil or steam the cauliflower florets until they get tender, about 8-10 minutes. Drain well and put aside.<br>3. Using a saucepan, melt the butter over moderate heat. Stir in the flour and prepare for 1 minute until bubbly. Gradually whisk in the milk. Season with salt and pepper. Continue cooking until the sauce gets thickened, about 5 minutes.<br>4. After taking the sauce from the heat, add the Gruyère cheese and stir until it has melted.<br>5. Arrange the cauliflower in a baking dish. Pour the cheese sauce over the cauliflower. Sprinkle with Parmesan cheese.<br>6. Bake for 20-25 minutes until the top is golden brown and bubbly.<br>7. Let it cool for a few minutes before serving. |

# FLAMICHE (LEEK TART)

**Prep Time:**
**20 mins**

**Cook Time:**
**45 mins**

**Serving**
**6**

**Nutrition:**    Calories: 395, Fat: 28g, Carbohydrates: 30g, Fiber: 2g, Protein: 8g

| INGREDIENTS | PREPARATIONS |
|---|---|
| 1 sheet puff pastry<br>4 large-sized leeks, white and light green parts only, thinly sliced<br>3 tablespoons unsalted butter<br>2 eggs<br>1/2 cup crème fraîche<br>Salt and black pepper to taste<br>1/4 teaspoon grated nutmeg | 1. Set the oven's heat to 375°F (190°C). Roll out the puff pastry and gently place it into a 9-inch tart pan to make a tart.<br>2. In a large-sized skillet, melt the butter over medium heat. Add the leeks and prepare until softened, about 10 minutes. Let it cool slightly.<br>3. In a bowl, whisk together the eggs and crème fraîche. Season with salt, pepper, and nutmeg. Stir in the cooled leeks.<br>4. Pour the leek blending into the tart shell.<br>5. Bake for 30-35 minutes until the filling is set and the top is golden brown.<br>6. Let it cool for a few minutes before slicing and serving. |

# MOULES MARINIÈRES (MUSSELS IN WHITE WINE)

**Prep Time:
10 mins**

**Cook Time:
20 mins**

**Serving
4**

**Nutrition:**   Calories: 210, Fat: 8g, Carbohydrates: 9g, Fiber: 0g, Protein: 14g

| INGREDIENTS | PREPARATIONS |
|---|---|
| 2 pounds fresh mussels, cleaned and de-bearded<br>2 tablespoons butter<br>2 shallots, finely chopped<br>2 cloves garlic, minced<br>1 cup dry white wine<br>1/2 cup chopped fresh parsley<br>Salt and black pepper to taste | 1. In a large-sized pot, melt the butter over moderate heat. Add the shallots and garlic and prepare until softened, about 3 minutes.<br>2. Add the wine and take it to a simmer. Add the mussels, cover the pot, and prepare until the mussels open, about 5-7 minutes. Discard any mussels that do not open.<br>3. Add the parsley to the mixture, then season it with salt and pepper.<br>4. Serve the mussels with the cooking liquid. |

# RATTE POTATOES WITH HERBS DE PROVENCE

**Prep Time:**
**10 mins**

**Cook Time:**
**35 mins**

**Serving**
**4**

**Nutrition:**   Calories: 220, Fat: 7g, Carbohydrates: 37g, Fiber: 4g, Protein: 5g

| INGREDIENTS | PREPARATIONS |
|---|---|
| 1.5 pounds Ratte or any small new potatoes<br>2 tablespoons olive oil<br>1 teaspoon Herbs de Provence<br>Salt and black pepper to taste<br>Freshly chopped parsley for garnish | 1. Set the oven's heat to 400°F (200°C).<br>2. Toss the potatoes with olive oil, Herbs de Provence, salt, and pepper.<br>3. Spread the potatoes on a cooking sheet in a single layer.<br>4. Roast for 30-35 minutes until the potatoes are golden brown and crisp. Stir halfway through for even roasting.<br>5. Sprinkle with chopped parsley before serving. |

# SPINACH AND GRUYÈRE SOUFFLÉ

**Prep Time:**
**20 mins**

**Cook Time:**
**30 mins**

**Serving**
**4**

**Nutrition:**   Calories: 370, Fat: 25g, Carbohydrates: 12g, Fiber: 1g, Protein: 23g

| INGREDIENTS | PREPARATIONS |
|---|---|
| 2 cups fresh spinach, finely chopped<br>4 tablespoons butter<br>1/4 cup all-purpose flour<br>1 1/4 cups whole milk<br>1/2 teaspoon nutmeg<br>Salt and black pepper to taste<br>1 cup Gruyère cheese, grated<br>4 large eggs separated | 1. Set the oven's heat to 375°F (190°C).<br>2. Using a saucepan, melt the butter over moderate heat. Add the flour and make a roux while gradually whisking in the milk. Cook until thickened, about 2-3 minutes.<br>3. Avoid heat and stir in the spinach, nutmeg, cheese, and egg yolks. Season with salt and pepper.<br>4. Vigorously whisk the egg whites in a separate bowl until they reach a stiff peak consistency. Gently fold into the spinach mixture.<br>5. Pour the mixture into a greased soufflé dish and bake for 25-30 minutes or until puffed and gets golden. Serve immediately. |

# SALADE DE LENTILLES (LENTIL SALAD)

**Prep Time:**
**15 mins**

**Cook Time:**
**30 mins**

**Serving**
**4**

**Nutrition:**    Calories: 320, Fat: 14g, Carbohydrates: 33g, Fiber: 16g, Protein: 13g

| INGREDIENTS | PREPARATIONS |
|---|---|
| 1 cup green lentils<br>1 bay leaf<br>2 cloves garlic, peeled<br>1 small red onion, finely chopped<br>2 tablespoons Dijon mustard<br>3 tablespoons red wine vinegar<br>1/4 cup extra-virgin olive oil<br>Salt and black pepper to taste<br>2 tablespoons finely chopped fresh parsley<br>1 freshly chopped tomato<br>1 diced avocado | 1. To prepare the lentils, grab a saucepan and combine them with bay leaf, garlic, and enough water to cover them by 2 inches. Take to a boil, turn the heat, and simmer until lentils are tender for about 25-30 minutes. Drain and discard the bay leaf and garlic.<br>2. Whisk together the mustard, vinegar, olive oil, salt, and pepper in a large bowl to make a vinaigrette.<br>3. Place the cooked lentils into the bowl containing the vinaigrette, chopped tomatoes and avocado. Stir in the red onion and parsley. Toss well to combine.<br>4. Serve warm or at room temperature. |

# BRANDADE DE MORUE (SALT COD AND POTATO PURÉE)

**Prep Time:**
**2 hour 15**
**mins**

**Cook Time:**
**40 mins**

**Serving**
**4**

**Nutrition:** Calories: 460, Fat: 27g, Carbohydrates: 23g, Fiber: 2g, Protein: 30g

| INGREDIENTS | PREPARATIONS |
|---|---|
| 1 pound salt cod<br>1 cup milk<br>2 large russet potatoes, peeled and cubed<br>3 cloves garlic, minced<br>1/2 cup extra-virgin olive oil<br>Salt and white pepper to taste | 1. To prepare salt cod, soak it in cold water for 24 hours and changing the water out, 4 or 5 times.<br>2. In a saucepan, combine the soaked cod and milk. Bring to a simmer and cook until the fish gets easily flaked with a fork, about 20 minutes. Drain, reserving the milk, and flake the fish.<br>3. Using another saucepan, boil the potatoes until tender, about 15 minutes. Drain.<br>4. Mash the potatoes and garlic together, then mix in the flaked cod. Gradually add the olive oil and enough reserved milk to achieve a creamy texture.<br>5. Season with salt and white pepper. Serve warm. |

# RABBIT IN MUSTARD SAUCE

**Prep Time:
15 mins**

**Cook Time:
1 hour**

**Serving
4**

**Nutrition:** Calories: 520, Fat: 32g, Carbohydrates: 5g, Fiber: 1g, Protein: 45g

| INGREDIENTS | PREPARATIONS |
|---|---|
| 1 rabbit, cut into pieces<br>Salt and black pepper to taste<br>2 tablespoons olive oil<br>4 cloves garlic, minced<br>1 cup white wine<br>1 cup chicken broth<br>2 tablespoons Dijon mustard<br>2 tablespoons grainy mustard<br>1/2 cup heavy cream<br>2 tablespoons chopped fresh parsley | 1. Add salt and pepper to the rabbit pieces.<br>2. In a large-sized pan, heat the oil over medium-high heat. Add the rabbit and brown on each side. Remove from the pan and set aside.<br>3. In the same pan, sauté the garlic until fragrant. To deglaze the pan, pour the wine and use a spatula to scrape the bottom.<br>4. Stir in the chicken broth and mustard. Return the rabbit to the pan and reduce the heat to low. Cover and simmer until the rabbit gets tender, about 45 minutes.<br>5. Stir in the heavy cream and parsley. Cook for another 5 minutes. Adjust the seasoning if necessary.<br>6. Serve the rabbit with the mustard sauce. |

# RÔTI DE PORC AU LAIT (PORK ROAST WITH MILK)

**Prep Time:**
**10 mins**

**Cook Time:**
**2 hour**

**Serving**
**6**

**Nutrition:**   Calories: 380, Fat: 20g, Carbohydrates: 6g, Fiber: 0g, Protein: 44g

| INGREDIENTS | PREPARATIONS |
|---|---|
| 2-pound pork loin roast<br>Salt and black pepper to taste<br>2 tablespoons vegetable oil<br>2 cloves garlic, peeled<br>4 cups whole milk<br>1 bay leaf<br>1 teaspoon dried thyme<br>Dried cranberries<br>Mixed nuts, finely chopped | 1. To prepare the pork loin, add salt and pepper for seasoning.<br>2. Heat the oil in a large-sized oven-safe pot over moderate-high heat. Put the pork loin in the pan and sear it until all sides are browned.<br>3. Add the garlic cloves, milk, bay leaf, and thyme. Turn the heat to low, cover, and simmer for 1 hour.<br>4. Adjust the oven to 350°F (175°C). Uncover the pot and transfer it to the preheated oven. Prepare the pork in the oven for 1 hour or until it is fully cooked.<br>5. Sprinkle the dried cranberries and nuts over the loin and allow the pork to sit for 10 mins before slicing. Serve with the milk sauce from the pot. |

# TARTE AU MAROILLES (MAROILLES CHEESE TART)

**Prep Time:**
**15 mins**

**Cook Time:**
**35 mins**

**Serving**
**6**

**Nutrition:**   Calories: 500, Fat: 36g, Carbohydrates: 28g, Fiber: 1g, Protein: 19g

| INGREDIENTS | PREPARATIONS |
|---|---|
| 1 1/2 cups all-purpose flour<br>1/2 cup cold butter, cubed<br>1/2 teaspoon salt<br>4-5 tablespoons cold water<br>1 pound Maroilles cheese, sliced<br>1 cup crème fraîche<br>2 eggs<br>1/4 teaspoon nutmeg<br>Black pepper to taste | 1. In a large-sized bowl, combine the flour, butter, and salt. To achieve a coarse breadcrumb-like texture, blend the butter and flour.<br>2. Gradually add the cold water, stirring until a dough forms. Please wrap the item in plastic and refrigerate it for one hour.<br>3. Set the oven's heat to 375°F (190°C). On a floured surface, roll out the dough and fit it into a nine-inch tart pan.<br>4. Arrange the Maroilles cheese slices over the dough.<br>5. Whisk together the crème fraîche, eggs, nutmeg, and black pepper in a bowl. Pour over the cheese.<br>6. Bake for 30-35 minutes or until the crust is golden and the filling is set. Let cool slightly before serving. |

# TARTE NORMANDE (APPLE CUSTARD TART)

**Prep Time:**
20 mins

**Cook Time:**
50 mins

**Serving**
8

**Nutrition:**    Calories: 360, Fat: 21g, Carbohydrates: 35g, Fiber: 2g, Protein: 5g

| INGREDIENTS | PREPARATIONS |
|---|---|
| 1 ready-made pie crust<br>3 large apples, slice through the core, then use a mandolin or peeler, to get thin, rollable slices<br>1/2 cup sugar<br>3 eggs<br>1 cup heavy cream<br>1 teaspoon vanilla extract<br>1/4 teaspoon cinnamon<br>Powdered sugar for dusting | 1. Set the oven's heat to 350°F (175°C). To make the tart, first put the pie crust into the tart pan and then carefully arrange the apple slices on top.<br>2. Sprinkle the sugar evenly over the apples.<br>3. Whisk together the eggs, heavy cream, vanilla extract, and cinnamon in a bowl. Pour over the apples.<br>4. The baking process should take around 45-50 minutes or until the filling has set and the crust has turned golden.<br>5. After allowing it to cool down, sprinkle powdered sugar before serving. |

# ENDIVE AND HAM GRATIN

**Prep Time:**
**20 mins**

**Cook Time:**
**25 mins**

**Serving**
**4**

**Nutrition:** Calories: 400, Fat: 25g, Carbohydrates: 15g, Fiber: 4g, Protein: 28g

| INGREDIENTS | PREPARATIONS |
|---|---|
| 4 Belgian endives, halved lengthwise<br>8 slices ham<br>2 cups béchamel sauce<br>1 cup grated Gruyère cheese<br>Salt and pepper to taste | 1. Set the oven's heat to 375°F (190°C). Grease a baking dish with butter.<br>2. Blanch the endives in boiling water for 10 minutes, then drain.<br>3. Wrapping a slice of ham around each half of the endive. Then, put them in the baking dish that has been prepared.<br>4. Pour the béchamel sauce over the endives and sprinkle with the cheese.<br>5. Prepare for 20-25 minutes or until the cheese is golden and bubbly. Season with salt and pepper before serving. |

# GRILLED TROUT WITH ALMONDS

**Prep Time:**
**10 mins**

**Cook Time:**
**10 mins**

**Serving**
**4**

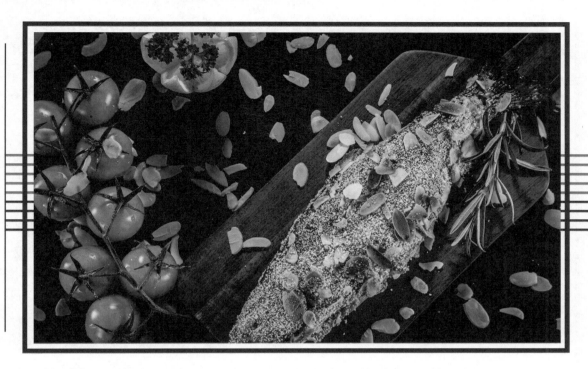

**Nutrition:** Calories: 360, Fat: 25g, Carbohydrates: 4g, Fiber: 2g, Protein: 30g

| INGREDIENTS | PREPARATIONS |
|---|---|
| 4 whole trout, cleaned and gutted<br>Salt and pepper to taste<br>4 tablespoons unsalted butter<br>1/2 cup sliced almonds<br>1 tablespoon chopped fresh parsley<br>1 lemon, sliced | 1. Preheat a grill or grill pan to medium heat.<br>2. Remember to season the trout's inside and outside with salt and pepper.<br>3. Grill the trout on each side for 4-5 minutes until the skin is crispy and the fish is cooked.<br>4. At the same time, heat a pan on moderate heat and melt the butter in it. Add the almonds and cook until golden, then stir in the parsley.<br>5. Serve the trout with the almond butter poured over top and lemon slices on the side. |

# CREAM OF CHESTNUT SOUP

**Prep Time:**
**10 mins**

**Cook Time:**
**30 mins**

**Serving**
**4**

**Nutrition:**   Calories: 480, Fat: 26g, Carbohydrates: 54g, Fiber: 2g, Protein: 7g

| INGREDIENTS | PREPARATIONS |
|---|---|
| 1 tablespoon olive oil<br>1 onion, chopped<br>2 cloves garlic, minced<br>1 lb roasted chestnuts, peeled<br>4 cups chicken or vegetable broth<br>1 cup heavy cream<br>Salt and pepper to taste<br>Fresh thyme leaves for garnish | 1. Heat the oil in a large-sized pot over medium heat. Add the onion, garlic, and sauté until the onions are translucent, about 5 minutes.<br>2. Add the chestnuts and broth and bring to a boil. Turn the heat and simmer for about 20 minutes until the chestnuts are tender.<br>3. Use a blender to puree the soup to achieve a smooth consistency. Return to the pot, stir in the cream, and season with salt and pepper.<br>4. Serve the soup garnished with fresh thyme leaves. |

# RABBIT TERRINE WITH PISTACHIOS

**Prep Time:**
**20 mins**

**Cook Time:**
**2 hour**

**Serving**
**8**

**Nutrition:**   Calories: 460, Fat: 32g, Carbohydrates: 6g, Fiber: 2g, Protein: 35g

| INGREDIENTS | PREPARATIONS |
| --- | --- |
| 1 lb rabbit meat, deboned<br>1/2 lb pork belly<br>1/2 lb chicken liver<br>1/2 cup pistachios<br>2 cloves garlic, minced<br>2 tablespoons brandy<br>Salt and pepper to taste<br>Fresh herbs for garnish | 1. Adjust your oven to 325°F (165°C). Combine the rabbit meat, pork belly, and chicken liver in a food processor. Pulse until finely chopped.<br>2. Transfer the blend to a bowl, add the pistachios, garlic, brandy, salt, and pepper. Mix until well combined.<br>3. Press the blending into a loaf pan or terrine mold, cover it with foil, and place it in a larger roasting pan. To prepare, pour boiling water into the roasting pan; fill the loaf pan halfway up the sides.<br>4. Bake for about 2 hours or until the terrine is firm to the touch. Let cool completely before slicing and serving, garnished with fresh herbs. |

# RATATOUILLE NIÇOISE

**Prep Time:**
**15 mins**

**Cook Time:**
**45 mins**

**Serving**
**4-6**

**Nutrition:**   Calories: 180, Fat: 11g, Carbohydrates: 20g, Fiber: 7g, Protein: 3g

| INGREDIENTS | PREPARATIONS |
|---|---|
| 1 large eggplant, diced<br>2 zucchini, diced<br>1 red bell pepper, diced<br>1 yellow bell pepper, diced<br>1 onion, chopped<br>4 cloves garlic, minced<br>4 large ripe tomatoes, chopped<br>1/4 cup olives, pitted and chopped<br>2 tablespoons capers<br>1/4 cup olive oil<br>1 tablespoon fresh thyme leaves<br>Salt and pepper to taste<br>Fresh basil leaves for garnish | 1. In a large-sized pan, heat the olive oil over medium heat. Add the eggplant, zucchini, and bell peppers. Cook until they start to soften.<br>2. Add the onion and garlic, and continue preparing until the onion is translucent.<br>3. Stir in the tomatoes, olives, capers, and thyme—season with salt and pepper. Lower the heat and allow to simmer for about 30 minutes or until the vegetables are tender and the flavors have melded together.<br>4. Garnish with fresh basil leaves before serving. |

# CERVELLE DE CANUT (HERBED CHEESE SPREAD)

**Prep Time:**
**10 mins**

**Cook Time:**
**2 hour**

**Serving**
**6**

**Nutrition:**   Calories: 100, Fat: 7g, Carbohydrates: 4g, Fiber: 0g, Protein: 6g

| INGREDIENTS | PREPARATIONS |
|---|---|
| 2 cups fromage blanc or Greek yogurt<br>3 tablespoons finely chopped fresh chives<br>3 tablespoons finely chopped fresh parsley<br>2 cloves garlic, minced<br>1 tablespoon white wine vinegar<br>2 tablespoons olive oil<br>Salt and pepper to taste | 1. Combine the fromage blanc/ Greek yogurt, chives, parsley, garlic, vinegar, and oil in a bowl. Mix until well combined.<br>2. Season with salt and pepper to taste.<br>3. It is recommended to refrigerate the spread for at least 2 hours before serving to ensure the flavors blend well. Serve with crusty bread or crackers. |

# FLAUGNARDE (BERRY CLAFOUTIS)

**Prep Time:**
**15 mins**

**Cook Time:**
**40 mins**

**Serving**
**6**

**Nutrition:** Calories: 180, Fat: 3g, Carbohydrates: 34g, Fiber: 2g, Protein: 6g, Sodium: 70mg

| INGREDIENTS | PREPARATIONS |
|---|---|
| 2 cups mixed berries (like blueberries, raspberries, and blackberries) <br> 1/2 cup granulated sugar <br> 3 large eggs <br> 1 cup whole milk <br> 1/2 cup all-purpose flour <br> 1 teaspoon vanilla extract <br> Pinch of salt <br> Powdered sugar for dusting | 1. Set your oven's heat to 375°F (190°C). Grease a round baking dish and add the mixed berries. <br> 2. Whisk together the sugar and eggs until they are well combined. Add the milk, flour, vanilla extract, and salt. Whisk until smooth. <br> 3. Pour the mixture over the berries into the baking dish. <br> 4. Bake the flaugnarde for approximately 40 minutes until it is puffed and golden, and a clean knife inserted in the center confirms it is cooked through. <br> 5. Let it cool slightly before dusting it with powdered sugar. Serve warm. |

# PETITS FARÇIS NIÇOIS (STUFFED VEGETABLES)

**Prep Time:**
20 mins

**Cook Time:**
1 hour

**Serving
6**

**Nutrition:**   Calories: 350, Fat: 20g, Carbohydrates: 17g, Fiber: 3g, Protein: 24g

| INGREDIENTS | PREPARATIONS |
|---|---|
| 6 small bell peppers<br>2 zucchini<br>2 tomatoes<br>1 onion, finely chopped<br>2 cloves garlic, minced<br>1/2 pound ground pork<br>1/2 pound ground beef<br>1/4 cup cooked rice<br>1/4 cup fresh parsley, chopped<br>1/4 cup fresh basil, chopped<br>1 egg<br>Salt and pepper to taste<br>Olive oil for drizzling | 1. Set your oven's heat to 350°F (175°C). Cut off the tops of the peppers, zucchini, and tomatoes. Scoop out the insides, then cut them in half and set aside.<br>2. Mix the onion, garlic, ground pork, beef, rice, parsley, basil, and egg in a large bowl—season with salt and pepper.<br>3. Stuff the vegetables with the meat mixture, replace the tops, and place them in a baking dish. Drizzle with olive oil.<br>4. Prepare for about 1 hour until the vegetables get tender and the meat is cooked. |

# PAN BAGNAT (PROVENÇAL TUNA SANDWICH)

**Prep Time:**
20 mins

**Cook Time:**
00 mins

**Serving**
4

**Nutrition:**   Calories: 460, Fat: 20g, Carbohydrates: 45g, Fiber: 5g, Protein: 25g

| INGREDIENTS | PREPARATIONS |
|---|---|
| 1 large round rustic bread loaf<br>1 can (5 oz) tuna in oil, drained<br>1/2 red onion, thinly sliced<br>1 large ripe tomato, sliced<br>1 small cucumber, sliced<br>1/2 cup black olives, pitted<br>2 hard-boiled eggs, sliced<br>4 anchovy fillets<br>1/4 cup extra-virgin olive oil<br>2 tablespoons red wine vinegar<br>Salt and pepper to taste | 1. Slice the bread loaf in half horizontally. Scoop out some of the bread from the center to make room for the filling.<br>2. Arrange the tuna, onion, tomato, cucumber, olives, eggs, and anchovies on the bottom half of the bread. To season, drizzle olive oil and red wine vinegar over the dish and sprinkle salt and pepper on top.<br>3. Top with the other half of the bread and press down gently. Wrap the sandwich tightly in plastic wrap and let it sit at room temperature for about 2 hours before serving. |

# CHÈVRE CHAUD SUR TOAST

**Prep Time:**
**10 mins**

**Cook Time:**
**10 mins**

**Serving**
**4**

**Nutrition:**   Calories: 240, Fat: 12g, Carbohydrates: 23g, Fiber: 2g, Protein: 10g

| INGREDIENTS | PREPARATIONS |
|---|---|
| 4 slices of rustic bread<br>4 ounces of goat cheese<br>1 tablespoon honey<br>1 tablespoon chopped fresh thyme<br>1 tablespoon olive oil<br>Salt and pepper to taste<br>Mixed greens for serving | 1. To start baking, make sure your oven is heated to 350°F (175°C). Lay the bread pieces on a cooking sheet.<br>2. Slice the goat cheese and place it on the bread slices. Drizzle with honey and sprinkle with thyme. Season with salt and pepper.<br>3. Drizzle olive oil over the bread and bake for 10 minutes or until the cheese is warm and slightly melted.<br>4. Serve the toast on a bed of mixed greens. |

# BRIOCHE FRENCH TOAST WITH LAVENDER HONEY

**Prep Time:
10 mins**

**Cook Time:
20 mins**

**Serving
4**

**Nutrition:**   Calories: 520, Fat: 25g, Carbohydrates: 60g, Fiber: 2g, Protein: 15g

| INGREDIENTS | PREPARATIONS |
|---|---|
| 8 slices brioche bread<br>4 eggs<br>1 cup milk<br>1 teaspoon vanilla extract<br>1/2 teaspoon lavender buds, crushed<br>1/4 cup honey<br>Butter for frying<br>Powdered sugar for dusting<br>Cup of mixed fruit | 1. Whisk together the eggs, milk, and vanilla extract in a large bowl.<br>2. Thoroughly coat the brioche slices by dipping them in the egg mixture.<br>3. Melt some butter in a large-sized non-stick skillet over medium heat. Add the soaked brioche slices and cook until golden brown on both sides, about 2-3 minutes per side.<br>4. Warm the honey and lavender buds over low heat in a small saucepan. Drizzle the lavender honey over the Serve French toast and sprinkle powdered sugar and mixed fruit over before serving. |

# MONT D'OR AU FOUR (BAKED MONT D'OR CHEESE)

**Prep Time:**
**15 mins**

**Cook Time:**
**25 mins**

**Serving**
**4**

**Nutrition:**   Calories: 460, Fat: 35g, Carbohydrates: 5g, Fiber: 0g, Protein: 28g

| INGREDIENTS | PREPARATIONS |
|---|---|
| 1 Mont d'Or cheese (about 500g) in its wooden box<br>2 cloves garlic, sliced<br>1 sprig of fresh rosemary<br>1/2 cup white wine<br>Baguette slices for serving | 1. Set your oven's heat to 350°F (175°C). Remove any plastic or paper packaging from the cheese but keep it in its wooden box.<br>2. Make several slits on the top of the cheese and insert the garlic slices. Place the rosemary sprig on top.<br>3. Pour the wine over the cheese. Bake for about 25 minutes or until the cheese is melted and bubbling.<br>4. Serve the baked cheese with baguette slices for dipping. |

# TOURNEDOS ROSSINI (BEEF WITH FOIE GRAS)

**Prep Time:**
**10 mins**

**Cook Time:**
**15 mins**

**Serving**
**4**

**Nutrition:**   Calories: 720, Fat: 55g, Carbohydrates: 10g, Fiber: 0g, Protein: 46g

| INGREDIENTS | PREPARATIONS |
| --- | --- |
| 4 beef filet mignon steaks<br>Salt and freshly ground pepper to taste<br>4 slices foie gras<br>2 tablespoons butter<br>4 pieces of baguette, toasted<br>1/2 cup Madeira wine<br>1/2 cup beef stock<br>2 sliced potatoes | 1. Lightly roast the sliced potatoes for around 20 minutes, meanwhile, season the steaks with salt and pepper. To cook the steaks to your preferred level of doneness, melt a tablespoon of butter in a heated skillet and then sear the steaks. Remove from skillet and keep warm.<br>2. In the same skillet, sear the foie gras slices on each side until golden brown, about 1-2 minutes per side. Remove from skillet and set aside.<br>3. Deglaze the skillet with Madeira wine, then add the beef stock. Reduce until thickened to make a sauce.<br>4. To serve, take a slice of toasted baguette and place a steak on top. Add a piece of foie gras on the steak, place on the sliced potatoes and then spoon the sauce over everything. Enjoy! |

# GALETTE COMPLÈTE

**Prep Time:**
**15 mins**

**Cook Time:**
**20 mins**

**Serving**
**4**

**Nutrition:**    Calories: 370, Fat: 20g, Carbohydrates: 25g, Fiber: 3g, Protein: 23g

| INGREDIENTS | PREPARATIONS |
|---|---|
| 1 cup buckwheat flour<br>1 egg<br>1/2 teaspoon salt<br>1 1/2 cups water<br>Butter for frying.<br>4 slices of ham<br>4 eggs<br>1 cup grated cheese | 1. Combine the buckwheat flour, egg, salt, and water in a bowl. Whisk until smooth.<br>2. Heat a non-stick pan over moderate heat and add a little butter.<br>3. Pour one-fourth of the batter into the pan and swirl it to distribute it evenly.<br>4. Cook until the edges lift from the pan, about 2-3 minutes. Flip and cook for another minute.<br>5. Place a slice of ham, an egg, and some cheese on one half of the crepe. Fold the other half over the top and cook until the cheese gets melted and the egg is cooked to your liking. Repeat with the remaining ingredients. |

# TARTINE PROVENÇALE

**Prep Time:**
**10 mins**

**Cook Time:**
**10 mins**

**Serving**
**4**

**Nutrition:**   Calories: 190, Fat: 7g, Carbohydrates: 27g, Fiber: 3g, Protein: 5g

| INGREDIENTS | PREPARATIONS |
|---|---|
| 4 slices of rustic bread<br>1 clove garlic<br>2 tablespoons olive oil<br>1 bell pepper, sliced<br>2 tomatoes, sliced<br>Salt and pepper to taste<br>Fresh basil leaves for garnish<br>Half a cup of Crumbled feta cheese | 1. Preheat the grill or broiler.<br>2. To make the bread slices crunchy and golden, grill or toast them on both sides.<br>3. To prepare, rub one side of each slice with a garlic clove and then drizzle some olive oil on top.<br>4. Sprinkle the feta over each slice, then a rrange the sliced bell pepper and tomatoes on top of each slice. Season with salt and pepper.<br>5. Return to the grill or broiler and cook until the vegetables are slightly charred.<br>6. Garnish with fresh basil leaves before serving. |

# SALADE DE MÂCHE (LAMB'S LETTUCE SALAD)

**Prep Time:**
**10 mins**

**Cook Time:**
**00 mins**

**Serving**
**4**

**Nutrition:**    Calories: 100, Fat: 10g, Carbohydrates: 2g, Fiber: 1g, Protein: 1g

| INGREDIENTS | PREPARATIONS |
|---|---|
| 6 cups of mâche (lamb's lettuce)<br>1 shallot, finely chopped<br>3 tablespoons olive oil<br>1 tablespoon white wine vinegar<br>Salt and pepper to taste | 1. Rinse the mâche thoroughly and pat dry.<br>2. Combine the chopped shallot, olive oil, and white wine vinegar in a bowl. Whisk to create a vinaigrette, and season with salt and pepper.<br>3. Toss the mâche with the vinaigrette until evenly coated.<br>4. Serve immediately. |

# SMOKED SALMON QUICHE

**Prep Time:**
**15 mins**

**Cook Time:**
**45 mins**

**Serving**
**6**

**Nutrition:**   Calories: 420, Fat: 30g, Carbohydrates: 20g, Fiber: 1g, Protein: 16g

## INGREDIENTS

1 pre-made pie crust
200g smoked salmon, chopped
4 large eggs
1 cup heavy cream
1 cup milk
Salt and pepper to taste
1 tablespoon fresh dill, chopped
1/2 cup grated Gruyère cheese
1 cup of small broccoli florets

## PREPARATIONS

1. Set the oven's heat to 375°F (190°C). Set the pie crust in a tart pan and prick the bottom with a fork.
2. Distribute the chopped smoked salmon and broccoli  evenly over the bottom of the pie crust.
3. Whisk together the eggs, cream, milk, salt, and pepper in a bowl. Stir in the chopped dill.
4. Pour the egg mixture over the salmon in the pie crust.
5. Sprinkle the Gruyère cheese on top.
6. Bake the quiche for 35-40 minutes or until it is fully set and has a golden appearance.
7. Let it cool for a few minutes before serving.

# DUCK BREAST WITH CHERRY SAUCE

**Prep Time:**
**15 mins**

**Cook Time:**
**30 mins**

**Serving**
**4**

**Nutrition:**  Calories: 450, Fat: 20g, Carbohydrates: 25g, Fiber: 1g, Protein: 35g

| INGREDIENTS | PREPARATIONS |
|---|---|
| 2 duck breasts<br>Salt and pepper to taste<br>1 cup fresh or frozen cherries, pitted<br>1/2 cup red wine<br>1/4 cup sugar<br>1 tablespoon balsamic vinegar | 1. Crank the oven to 375°F (190°C). To prepare the duck breasts, use a sharp tool to score the skin, then season both sides with salt and pepper.<br>2. Warm a skillet over medium-high heat, and sear the duck breasts skin-side down for 5 minutes or until the skin gets golden and crispy. Turn the duck breasts and sear for another 2 minutes.<br>3. Transfer the duck breasts to the oven, and roast for 10 minutes for medium-rare.<br>4. Before starting to cook the duck, make sure to prepare the sauce. Combine the cherries, red wine, sugar, and balsamic vinegar in a saucepan. Please bring it to a simmer and prepare it until the sauce has reduced by half.<br>5. To serve, slice the duck breasts and accompany them with the cherry sauce. |

# LAMB NAVARIN

**Prep Time:**
**30 mins**

**Cook Time:**
**2 hour**

**Serving**
**6**

**Nutrition:**   Calories: 420, Fat: 20g, Carbohydrates: 14g, Fiber: 3g, Protein: 40g

| INGREDIENTS | PREPARATIONS |
|---|---|
| 2 lb lamb shoulder, cut into chunks<br>Salt and black pepper to taste<br>2 tbsp vegetable oil<br>2 cloves garlic, minced<br>1 onion, chopped<br>1 tbsp tomato paste<br>1 cup white wine<br>4 cups chicken stock<br>1 bouquet garni (thyme, bay leaf, and parsley tied together)<br>1 cup carrots<br>1 cup small turnips<br>1 cup green peas<br>Fresh parsley for garnish | 1. Season the lamb with salt and pepper. Heat the oil in a large pot over medium-high heat, then add the lamb and brown on all sides. Remove the lamb and set aside.<br>2. In the same pot, add the garlic and onion. Cook until softened.<br>3. Add the tomato paste and deglaze the pot with white wine, making sure to scrape up any light-browned bits from the bottom.<br>4. Return the lamb to the pot and add the chicken stock and bouquet garni. Take to a boil, then reduce to a simmer.<br>5. Cover and simmer for 1.5 hours or until the lamb is tender.<br>6. Add the carrots, turnips, and peas to the pot. Cook for another 15-20 minutes or until the vegetables are tender.<br>7. If desired, add salt & pepper to taste and serve the stew with fresh parsley as a garnish. |

# VEAL BLANQUETTE (VEAL IN WHITE SAUCE)

**Prep Time:**
30 mins

**Cook Time:**
2 hour

**Serving**
4

**Nutrition:** Calories: 500, Fat: 24g, Carbohydrates: 15g, Fiber: 2g, Protein: 54g

| INGREDIENTS | PREPARATIONS |
|---|---|
| 2 lb veal shoulder, cut into chunks<br>Salt and black pepper to taste<br>2 tbsp butter<br>1 onion, chopped<br>2 cloves garlic, minced<br>1 bay leaf<br>1 sprig of thyme<br>4 cups chicken stock<br>2 carrots, cut into chunks<br>2 celery sticks, cut into chunks<br>1/4 cup all-purpose flour<br>1/4 cup heavy cream<br>Chopped parsley for garnish<br>Half a cup of sliced mushrooms | 1. Season the veal with salt and pepper. In a large pot, melt the butter over medium-high heat, then add the veal and brown on all sides. Remove the veal and set aside.<br>2. Using the pot, add the onion and garlic. Cook until softened.<br>3. Return the veal to the pot and sprinkle with flour, stirring to coat the meat evenly.<br>4. Add the bay leaf, thyme, chicken stock, mushrooms, carrots, and celery. Take to a boil, then reduce to a simmer.<br>5. Cover and simmer for 1.5 hours or until the veal is tender.<br>6. After adding heavy cream, taste the dish and add salt & pepper if needed to adjust the seasoning.<br>7. Serve the blanquette garnished with chopped parsley. |

# BUCKWHEAT CREPES WITH HAM AND CHEESE

**Prep Time:**
**10 mins**

**Cook Time:**
**15 mins**

**Serving**
**4**

**Nutrition:** Calories: 350, Fat: 20g, Carbohydrates: 20g, Fiber: 2g, Protein: 22g

| INGREDIENTS | PREPARATIONS |
|---|---|
| 1 cup buckwheat flour<br>2 eggs<br>1/2 tsp salt<br>1 1/2 cups milk<br>2 tbsp butter, melted<br>4 slices of ham<br>1 cup grated Gruyère cheese | 1. Whisk together the buckwheat flour, eggs, salt, and half of the milk until smooth. Whisk in the rest of the milk and the melted butter. Allowing the batter to rest for at least one hour is essential.<br>2. Heat a non-stick skillet over medium heat. Pour one-fourth of the batter into the skillet and swirl it around until it covers the bottom. Cook for 1-2 minutes or until set and slightly browned.<br>3. Flip the crepe over and immediately lay a piece of ham and 1/4 cup of cheese on one half of the crepe. Fold the other half over the filling and press down gently.<br>4. Cook for another minute or until the cheese gets melted, then slide it onto a plate.<br>5. Repeat with the remaining batter and fillings. Serve immediately. |

# GRILLED MUSSELS WITH PARSLEY AND GARLIC

**Prep Time:**
**10 mins**

**Cook Time:**
**10 mins**

**Serving**
**4**

**Nutrition:**   Calories: 290, Fat: 16g, Carbohydrates: 10g, Fiber: 0g, Protein: 22g

| INGREDIENTS | PREPARATIONS |
|---|---|
| 2 lbs mussels, scrubbed and de-bearded<br>1/4 cup olive oil<br>4 cloves garlic, minced<br>1/2 cup chopped fresh parsley<br>1 lemon, cut into wedges | 1. Preheat a grill to medium-high heat. Place the mussels on the grill rack and close the lid. Cook for about 5 minutes or until the mussels have opened. Discard any that remain closed.<br>2. While the mussels are grilling, heat the olive oil in a small-sized saucepan over moderate heat. Add the garlic and prepare for 1-2 minutes, until fragrant but not browned. Remove from the heat and stir in the parsley.<br>3. When the mussels are ready, transfer them to a large bowl. Pour the garlic-parsley oil over the mussels and toss well. Serve right away with lemon wedges on the side for squeezing. |

# RED SNAPPER WITH TOMATO AND OLIVES

**Prep Time:**
**10 mins**

**Cook Time:**
**20 mins**

**Serving**
**4**

**Nutrition:** Calories: 280, Fat: 10gm, Carbohydrates: 7g, Fiber: 2g, Protein: 40g

| INGREDIENTS | PREPARATIONS |
|---|---|
| 4 red snapper fillets<br>Salt and pepper<br>2 tablespoons olive oil<br>1 onion, chopped<br>2 cloves garlic, minced<br>One can (14 oz) diced tomatoes<br>1/2 cup pitted black olives<br>1 tablespoon chopped fresh parsley | 1. Before cooking, season both sides of the snapper fillets with salt and pepper. Heat the olive oil in a large-sized skillet over medium-high heat. Add the snapper and prepare for 2 minutes per side or until lightly browned. Remove the snapper to a plate.<br>2. Using the same skillet, put in the onion and cook for 2-3 minutes or until it gets softened. Add the garlic and prepare for another minute.<br>3. Now it's time to add the tomatoes and juice and bring the mixture to a gentle simmer. Prepare for 5 minutes or until the tomatoes have broken down slightly.<br>4. Return the snapper to the skillet, nestling it into the tomato mixture. Scatter the olives over the top. Cover the skillet and prepare for 10 minutes or until the snapper is cooked.<br>5. Sprinkle with parsley before serving. |

DESSERT

# FIGS ROASTED WITH HONEY AND THYME

**Prep Time:
10 mins**

**Cook Time:
15 mins**

**Serving
4**

**Nutrition:**   Calories: 120, Fat: 0g, Carbohydrates: 31g, Fiber: 5g, Protein: 1g

| INGREDIENTS | PREPARATIONS |
|---|---|
| 12 fresh figs, cut in quarters, leaving a small amount at the base keeping the fig loosely connected<br>2 tablespoons honey<br>2 sprigs of fresh thyme<br>1/4 teaspoon sea salt<br>Zest and juice of 1 lemon | 1. Set your oven's heat to 375°F (190°C). Arrange fig cut-side up on a baking sheet<br>2. Drizzle the figs with honey, then sprinkle with thyme leaves, salt, and lemon zest.<br>3. Roast for 15 minutes or until the figs are tender and the honey caramelizes.<br>4. Remove from the oven, drizzle with fresh lemon juice, and serve warm. |

# PÂTE DE FRUITS (FRUIT JELLIES)

**Prep Time:**
**20 mins**

**Cook Time:**
**30 mins**

**Serving**
**36 piece**

**Nutrition:**   Calories: 40, Fat: 0g, Carbohydrates: 10g, Fiber: 0g, Protein: 0g

| INGREDIENTS | PREPARATIONS |
|---|---|
| 2 cups pure fruit juice<br>1 1/2 cups sugar<br>4 tablespoons pectin<br>Additional sugar for coating<br>2 cups pure fruit juice (per color) different juices will give different colors for layering; orange, line, strawberry, white/red grape juices are recommended. | 1. Combine the fruit juice, sugar, and pectin in a medium saucepan. Take to a boil over moderate heat, stirring constantly.<br>2. Continue boiling while stirring for about 15 minutes until the mixture thickens.<br>3. Pour the blending into a 9-inch square pan lined with parchment paper. Let cool to room temperature, then refrigerate until set, about 2 hours.<br>4. Cut the fruit jelly into 1-inch squares, layer with other colors as desired and roll in additional sugar before serving. |

# RED WINE POACHED PEARS

**Prep Time:**
**10 mins**

**Cook Time:**
**25 mins**

**Serving**
**4**

**Nutrition:**    Calories: 400, Fat: 0g, Carbohydrates: 70g, Fiber: 5g, Protein: 1g

| INGREDIENTS | PREPARATIONS |
|---|---|
| 4 ripe pears<br>750 ml red wine<br>1 cup sugar<br>1 cinnamon stick<br>2 star anise<br>1 vanilla pod | 1. Combine the red wine, sugar, cinnamon stick, star anise, and the seeds scraped from the vanilla pod in a large pot. Stir until the sugar dissolves.<br>2. Peel the pears, leaving the stem intact. Add them to the pot and bring to a simmer.<br>3. Cover the pot and let it simmer for about 20-25 minutes or until the pears are tender.<br>4. To take out the pears from the pot, use a slotted spoon. Continue simmering the poaching liquid until it reduces to syrup.<br>5. To serve, place each pear on a dessert plate and drizzle with the reduced syrup. |

# MOUSSE AU CHOCOLAT NOIR

**Prep Time:**
**20 mins**

**Cook Time:**
**2 hour**

**Serving**
**6**

**Nutrition:**  Calories: 280, Fat: 18g, Carbohydrates: 25g, Fiber: 2g, Protein: 6g

| INGREDIENTS | PREPARATIONS |
| --- | --- |
| 6 oz dark chocolate, chopped<br>4 eggs separated<br>1/4 cup sugar<br>Whipped cream and chocolate shavings for garnish | 1. To melt the chocolate, lay it in a heatproof bowl and set it over a pot of boiling water. Remove from heat and let cool slightly.<br>2. Whisk the egg yolks and sugar using a bowl until they become light and fluffy.<br>3. Vigorously whisk the egg whites in a separate bowl until they form stiff peaks.<br>4. Stir the egg yolk blending into the melted chocolate, then generously fold in the egg whites until no white streaks remain.<br>5. Transfer the mousse to individual serving dishes and place them in the refrigerator for at least two hours or until they are firm.<br>6. Serve the chocolate mousse garnished with whipped cream and chocolate shavings. |

# CARAMELIZED SHALLOT TART

**Prep Time:** 20 mins

**Cook Time:** 1 hour

**Serving** 6

**Nutrition:**   Calories: 450, Fat: 30g, Carbohydrates: 28g, Fiber: 2g, Protein: 12g

| INGREDIENTS | PREPARATIONS |
|---|---|
| 2 cups thinly sliced shallots<br>2 tablespoons olive oil<br>Salt and pepper to taste<br>1 tablespoon sugar<br>1 tablespoon balsamic vinegar<br>1 pre-made tart shell<br>2 eggs<br>1 cup heavy cream<br>1 cup shredded Gruyère cheese | 1. Adjust the oven's heat to 375°F (190°C).<br>2. In a pan, sauté the shallots in olive oil over medium heat until they soften. Season with salt and pepper.<br>3. Sprinkle sugar over the shallots, then cook until they get caramelized. After cooking, pour some balsamic vinegar into the pan and let it simmer until the liquid is reduced.<br>4. Spread the caramelized shallots over the bottom of the tart shell.<br>5. In a bowl, whisk together the eggs and cream. Pour this mixture over the shallots in the tart shell.<br>6. Sprinkle the Gruyère cheese on top.<br>7. Prepare for 30-35 minutes or until the tart is golden and the filling is set. |

# MADELEINES (FRENCH SPONGE CAKES)

**Prep Time:**
**15 mins**

**Cook Time:**
**12 mins**

**Serving**
**12**

**Nutrition:**   Calories: 140, Fat: 7g, Carbohydrates: 17g, Fiber: 0g, Protein: 2g

| INGREDIENTS | PREPARATIONS |
|---|---|
| 2 large eggs<br>2/3 cup granulated sugar<br>1 teaspoon vanilla extract<br>1/2 teaspoon lemon zest<br>1 cup all-purpose flour<br>1/2 cup unsalted butter, melted and chilled<br>Icing sugar for dusting | 1. Set your oven's temperature to 375°F (190°C) and grease a madeleine pan.<br>2. Whisk together the eggs, sugar, vanilla extract, and lemon zest until light and fluffy.<br>3. Gradually add the flour, whisking until smooth.<br>4. While whisking continuously, slowly add the cooled melted butter.<br>5. Fill each mold of the madeleine pan with the batter, making sure to fill it up to about 3/4.<br>6. Bake for 10-12 minutes or until the madeleines are golden brown.<br>7. After baking, it's best to let the madeleines cool for a few minutes inside the pan before moving them to a wire rack.<br>8. Dust with icing sugar before serving. |

# PARIS-BREST (CHOUX PASTRY WITH PRALINE CREAM)

**Prep Time:**
**30 mins**

**Cook Time:**
**35 mins**

**Serving**
**8**

**Nutrition:**   Calories: 400, Fat: 25g, Carbohydrates: 35g, Fiber: 1g, Protein: 7g

| INGREDIENTS | PREPARATIONS |
|---|---|
| For the choux pastry:<br>1 cup water<br>1/2 cup unsalted butter<br>1 cup all-purpose flour<br>4 large eggs<br>For the praline cream:<br>1 cup milk<br>1/4 cup sugar<br>2 egg yolks<br>2 tablespoons cornstarch<br>1/2 cup praline paste<br>1 cup heavy cream | 1. Set your's heat oven to 425°F (220°C). Draw an 8-inch circle on parchment paper, then place it on a baking sheet. In a pot, bring the water and butter to a boil. Take the mixture off the heat and swiftly mix in the flour until a dough is set up. After cracking open each egg, add it to the mixture and ensure it is thoroughly mixed before moving on to the next egg. The dough should be smooth and glossy.<br>2. Pipe the dough onto the parchment paper following the circle, making two rings side by side and one on top. Bake for 15 minutes, lower the oven heat to 375°F (190°C), and prepare for another 20 minutes. Allow the pastry to cool.<br>3. Meanwhile, make the praline cream. Begin by warming the milk in a pot until it starts to steam. Whisk together the sugar, egg yolks, and cornstarch in a separate bowl.<br>4. While whisking constantly, pour the hot milk gradually into the egg yolk mixture. Return the mixture to the pot and cook over medium heat, stirring continuously, until it thickens. Remove from heat and stir in the praline paste. Allow the cream to cool. First, whip the heavy cream until it reaches the soft peak stage. Next, carefully fold the whipped cream into the cooled praline cream.<br>5. Slice the cooled choux pastry in half horizontally. Pipe or spoon the praline cream onto the bottom half, then replace the top. Dust with icing sugar before serving. |

# POTATOES ANNA (LAYERED POTATO CAKE)

**Prep Time:**
**15 mins**

**Cook Time:**
**50 mins**

**Serving**
**4-6**

**Nutrition:**    Calories: 200, Fat: 7g, Carbohydrates: 32g, Fiber: 2g, Protein: 4g

| INGREDIENTS | PREPARATIONS |
|---|---|
| 2 lb russet potatoes, peeled and sliced<br>4 tbsp unsalted butter, melted<br>Salt and black pepper to taste | 1. Adjust your oven's heat to 425°F (220°C).<br>2. Arrange potato slices in a layer at the bottom of a round non-stick baking dish, overlapping slightly.<br>3. To prepare the potatoes, brush them with melted butter and add salt and pepper for seasoning.<br>4. Continue layering and seasoning the potatoes until all are used.<br>5. To cook the dish, cover it with foil and bake it for 30 minutes.<br>6. After removing the foil, bake the potatoes for 20 minutes until they turn golden and crispy.<br>7. Allow to cool for a few minutes before flipping onto a serving platter. Cut into wedges to serve. |

# MERINGUES WITH WHIPPED CREAM

**Prep Time:**
**20 mins**

**Cook Time:**
**60 mins**

**Serving**
**6**

**Nutrition:**   Calories: 250, Fat: 13g, Carbohydrates: 30g, Fiber: 0g, Protein: 4g

| INGREDIENTS | PREPARATIONS |
|---|---|
| 4 large egg whites<br>1 cup granulated sugar<br>1 tsp vanilla extract<br>1 cup heavy cream, whipped<br>1 tbsp powdered sugar<br>Fresh berries for serving | 1. Adjust your oven to 225°F (105°C) and place a cooking sheet with parchment paper.<br>2. Whisk the egg whites in a clean and dry bowl until soft peaks are formed.<br>3. Gradually add the sugar while beating the whites until they hold stiff peaks.<br>4. Fold in the vanilla extract.<br>5. Place six large dollops of meringue onto the cooking sheet that has been prepared in advance. Make a small well in the center of each dollop.<br>6. Bake for 60 minutes or until the meringues are crisp and dry. Allow to cool completely.<br>7. Whisk the heavy cream and powdered sugar tr until they reach a soft peak consistency.<br>8. Just before serving, fill the well in each meringue with cream and top with fresh berries. |

# CHERRY CLAFOUTIS

**Prep Time:**
**15 mins**

**Cook Time:**
**40 mins**

**Serving**
**8**

**Nutrition:**   Calories: 220, Fat: 3g, Carbohydrates: 45g, Fiber: 2g, Protein: 6g

| INGREDIENTS | PREPARATIONS |
|---|---|
| 1 lb fresh cherries, pitted<br>4 eggs<br>1 cup sugar<br>1 cup all-purpose flour<br>1 cup milk<br>1 teaspoon vanilla extract<br>Icing sugar for dusting | 1. Adjust your oven's temperature to 375°F (190°C). Butter a 9-inch pie dish and scatter the pitted cherries over the bottom.<br>2. In a bowl, whisk together the eggs and sugar until frothy. Whisk in the flour until it gets smooth, then slowly whisk in the milk and vanilla.<br>3. The next step is to pour the batter evenly over the cherries in the dish.<br>4. Prepare for 40-45 minutes until puffed and golden, and a tester enters the center and comes out clean.<br>5. Let cool slightly, then dust with icing sugar just before serving. |

# CHOCOLATE AND ALMOND TORTE

**Prep Time:**
**15 mins**

**Cook Time:**
**40 mins**

**Serving**
**8**

**Nutrition:** Calories: 400, Fat: 24g, Carbohydrates: 43g, Fiber: 4g, Protein: 7g

| INGREDIENTS | PREPARATIONS |
|---|---|
| 1 cup semi-sweet chocolate chips<br>1/2 cup butter<br>1 cup granulated sugar<br>3 eggs<br>1/2 cup cocoa powder<br>1 teaspoon vanilla extract<br>1/2 cup ground almonds | 1. Set the oven's temperature to 350°F (175°C) to bake. To prepare an 8-inch round baking pan, spread grease and put a piece of parchment paper at the bottom.<br>2. To melt the chocolate chips and butter, use a double boiler on low temperature and stir until smooth. Once melted, take it off the heat and let it cool down a bit.<br>3. Whisk together the sugar and eggs in a large-sized bowl until they become light and fluffy. Stir in the cocoa powder and vanilla extract until fully incorporated.<br>4. Gently whisk in the melted chocolate, blending until smooth. Fold in the ground almonds.<br>5. Pour the batter into the prepared cooking pan. Bake for 35-40 minutes, or until the tip of a toothpick inserted into the torte's center remains clean.<br>6. Allow the torte to sit in the pan for 10 minutes, take it out and let it cool completely on a wire rack. |

# Conclusion

As we reach the end of our journey through the charming avenues of French bistro cuisine, it is my hope that the essence of France – with its vibrant flavors, timeless traditions, and heartfelt stories – has resonated deeply within you. "Parisian Bistro Delights; Tastes of France" was crafted not merely as a cookbook but as an invitation into the soul of France, shared through its dishes

Each recipe we explored, from the simplest appetizer to the most elaborate entrée, embodies the spirit of a bistro: a warm embrace in every bite, a story whispered in every aroma. Perhaps you've come to understand that French cooking isn't just about ingredients or techniques; it's about passion, patience, and the love poured into each dish.

Whether you've chosen to replicate these dishes for a quiet evening at home, a festive family gathering, or a romantic dinner for two, know that you've added a touch of French magic to the occasion. These recipes aren't just meals; they're experiences waiting to be shared and memories waiting to be made.

As you continue your culinary adventures beyond this book, may the flavors of France linger on your palate, urging you to experiment, explore, and cherish the joys of cooking and sharing. And remember, the heart of bistro cooking lies not in perfection but in the love and authenticity you infuse in every dish.

Thank you for allowing me to be a part of your kitchen stories, and may every meal you craft from this book transport you to a quaint bistro, under the soft glow of Parisian lights.

Until our next gastronomic rendezvous, Bon Appétit!

Review Tastes of France